Spartan Discipline

Learn Spartan Techniques for Grow Your Mental Toughness

(How to Develop Spartan Discipline Unbreakable Mental Toughness and Relentless Willpower)

James Hayes

Published By **Darby Connor**

James Hayes

*Spartan Discipline: Learn Spartan Techniques for
Grow Your Mental Toughness (How to Develop
Spartan Discipline Unbreakable Mental Toughness
and Relentless Willpower)*

ISBN 978-1-998038-83-1

No part of this guidebook shall be reproduced in any form without permission in writing from the publisher except in the case of brief quotations embodied in critical articles or reviews.

Legal & Disclaimer

The information contained in this book is not designed to replace or take the place of any form of medicine or professional medical advice. The information in this book has been provided for educational & entertainment purposes only.

The information contained in this book has been compiled from sources deemed reliable, and it is accurate to the best of the Author's knowledge; however, the Author cannot guarantee its accuracy and validity and cannot be held liable for any errors or omissions. Changes are periodically made to this book. You must consult your doctor or get professional medical advice before using any of the suggested remedies, techniques, or information in this book.

Table Of Contents

Chapter 1: The Truth About Obstacles

Before jumping into the way to remove limitations, you require to understand the fact of them. Everybody is aware what a venture is, however maximum have an impractical and warped idea approximately it. Instead of viewing barriers as possibilities for boom, humans see them as sports running towards them. This unrealistic concept makes it some distance more tough to triumph over your assignment and alternate it into achievement.

With that in mind, you want to recognize the truth about barriers: challenges aren't all terrible. I understand this concept would probably sound a bit radical, however it holds. Similar to the whole lot else in lifestyles, obstacles include every positives and negatives. Recognizing every facets will help you to triumph over the obstacle abruptly and efficaciously.

Why Looking at Both the Negatives and Positives Matters

Whenever a barrier comes your way, it's far critical to preserve in thoughts this fact. If you simply recognition at the negatives, which the bulk of humans do, it's far an awful lot a great deal less complicated to get distraught, overloaded, and depressed through the situation. This will make it more tough to conquer the undertaking and flip it into achievement.

However, in case you observe the negatives and the positives, you observe the undertaking in masses greater reasonable moderate. This practical knowledge of obstacles permits you to suppose fairly and evidently about the venture available. From there, you can start to triumph over your obstacle as an alternative of having beaten via it.

Not to mention, you get rid of the majority of the negatives of disturbing conditions every time you view the positives. This will make it hundreds a great deal much less difficult and further high-quality to fight your traumatic situations, even if you are not usually succeeding as rapid as you would like.

Possible Negatives of Obstacles

Challenges embody numerous negatives. Even despite the reality which you should not get captured within the negatives, you have to be aware of them so that you apprehend a manner to amazing circulate approximately your scenario and eliminate the impediment. Whenever you understand the negatives, extra of the electricity is again to you.

As a result, you could begin to grasp the barrier due to the truth the negatives are your very very very own. Acknowledging them simply makes them less scary. The specific negatives of the assignment will rely on the mission. For instance, your task is probably coming across a brand-new task. In this situation, the negatives might be that you are beneath financial tension, require to transport, or a few element else associated with the actual challenge. These negatives are awesome from the negatives of numerous boundaries, like dating problems.

In addition to the task-focused negatives, a few negatives be successful in all barriers. Most specially, boundaries want you to work. If you've got were given already got a whole-time challenge and one-of-a-type responsibilities, the protected duty of having rid of the barrier can take a exquisite deal of a while and power, even for the most hardworking of human beings.

Not surely that, but obstacles assignment you bodily, mentally, and emotionally. Each time you discover your self in a brand-new barrier, you are required to venture your self to expand as a person. This manner uses up, all over again, a number of electricity, and it could convey up pretty some terrible feelings depending at the situation.

The wanted try and emotional turmoil that include the majority of limitations are what make obstacles so horrible. Most human beings do no longer like more art work. So, they broaden to dislike obstacles.

Ensured Positives of Obstacles

In addition to the negatives, obstacles have masses of positives. The majority of people stop working to appearance those positives, and that they give attention to the negatives instead. Though this is incredibly attractive to do, you have to try your hardest to keep the positives in your thoughts. The positives will will can help you remove the challenges, continue to be encouraged, and take satisfaction within the gadget.

Forces You to Grow

The biggest favorable of any mission is that it traumatic conditions you to amplify. Even despite the fact that obstacles come with a fantastic deal of hard paintings and try, it's far the best way in order to come to be the man or woman you need to be. In other terms, issues make you a higher man or woman.

Some disturbing situations may also make you physical higher, which include unrivaled fitness care, at the identical time as others will make you emotionally extra durable. It does now not depend variety how the assignment makes you grow. What subjects is which you grow and come to be a far better person on the quit of it all.

Helps You to Get to Know Yourself Better

Another advantage to coming out of boundaries is which you are familiar with yourself higher. We are frequently knowledgeable to get to understand our colleagues, relative, and buddies, however, we normally forget about to recognize ourselves. This makes it greater tough for us to simply accept as proper with our thoughts and understand what we want out of lifestyles.

Obstacles require us to mirror on ourselves and the sector. It teaches us our strengths, susceptible points, and boundaries. This lets in us to investigate more about ourselves in this sort of way that could not be viable without disturbing situations.

Enhances Self-Esteem

As we increase and examine more approximately ourselves masses better, our vanity grows additionally. So, demanding situations bring about accelerated vanity, that is their 0.33 benefit. Self-self belief is what permits us to understand our cost out of doors of our accomplishments and abilities. It is crucial for a extraordinarily joyful and working existence.

Improves Relationships

The last benefit of demanding situations is that they can beautify our relationships. You probably have seen that humans with shared hardships have a tendency to be a number of your maximum effective and maximum relied on relationships. As you go through demanding situations, you emerge as being greater records and in a function to talk with exclusive people in similar conditions.

Recap

All in all, worrying situations are not an entirely terrible difficulty. Even even though they'll be loads of paintings and might located pressure to your existence, they strain you to boom, will assist you to be familiar with yourself, enhance your arrogance, and enhance your relationships. Remembering those positives and the negatives will assist you do away with the assignment due to your practical and logical frame of mind.

Chapter 2: Perception Matters

Something that we cited within the last financial disaster however did now not explicitly speak is the problem of perception. Our understandings are how we interpret activities or individuals based totally upon our sensory reviews. Even although our perceptions are all we apprehend, how we apprehend an event may not be specific to the way it unfolds in fact.

Most likely sufficient, we are able to in no way leave our understandings, no matter how hard we attempt. Understandings adjust each single element of our regular life. How we view the region sooner or later identifies a number of our situations and emotions.

Because of how essential information is in our lifestyles, your notion of the obstacle will regularly emerge as aware of the manner you control it and whether or now not or now not you could conquer it. Enhance your perception of limitations to will let you flip any challenge proper right right into a achievement.

What the Psychology States About Understanding

Psychology has completed a excellent deal of studies have a take a look at on data. As we already stated, psychology figures out that our information is determined by way of manner of our sensory enjoy with the world, implying our enjoy of sight, scent, touch, and further.

More so, psychology has located that it determines how we react to our limitations. For example, if we adversely view obstacles, we are more likely to surrender and experience defeated by way of of using them. On the alternative hand, having an tremendous mind-set approximately the impediment makes us more likely to eliminate the project and prosper.

The most beneficial problem that psychology informs us approximately notion is that we've got some manipulate. Though it's miles impossible to have whole manipulate, we can a bit adjust our understandings with the aid of paying interest, purposefully turning our records into importance, appearing for this reason, and training with our new body of thoughts.

●Pay hobby: What is your perception of an occasion? How does it variety from reality? How do you recognize?

●Give your information significance: What does it indicate to you? Do you be given as genuine with this significance? Should you exchange the this means that?

•Act as a end result: How do my actions replicate my view of the situation?

•Practice: What are way ins which I can encompass this new united states of america of mind into my normal life?

What this indicates for annoying situations is that you can turn your unfavourable perception or frame of thoughts right into a high quality one. Just with planned and devoted action, you can discover your self much more likely to prosper through converting your mindset.

As you're actively looking to modify your mind-set, it's miles satisfactory to diploma your development with the useful resource of taking notes or the usage of some app. Continue to behave with the useful resource of this logo-new frame of thoughts and song your improvement. Stay nice even when it is difficult, and you'll begin to see your nation of a mind shift.

Popular Mindsets

Considering that knowledge topics, you're probable thinking what sort of a mindset you have to have. There are three famous states of thoughts, but handiest one will result in lengthy-term success. The steady body of thoughts, the blended body of mind, and the boom country of thoughts are all three well-known frames of mind that humans unwittingly have.

Fixed State of thoughts

The consistent nation of thoughts informs us that we're born with abilties and skills. We can not without a doubt surpass our talents, implying our achievement is surely as an lousy lot as our genetics. For instance, a fixed attitude need to assist you to know that you may never get a very good grade in school thinking about that you aren't clever.

This mind-set is quite famous, however, it's miles dangerous. It removes any energy over our conditions and blames it on our natural abilties. Not just that, however the repaired nation of thoughts is fake. In the instance talked about in the last paragraph, a student presumes they're capable of by no means get an superb grade thinking about the fact that they'll be no longer clever. Except for excessive learning disabilities, maximum trainees can get an awesome grade with difficult artwork and try, regardless of the fact that they aren't the most manifestly sensible. This indicates the fixed body of mind to be wrong.

Development State of mind

The opposite of the repaired state of mind is the growth frame of thoughts. The boom united states of thoughts tells you that you have certain herbal skills and strengths, but, you can nurture your prone factors and make bigger as a person. For instance, a increase kingdom of mind might also can help you recognise that you are not the finest at mathematics, but you may decorate with dedication and tough paintings.

The boom attitude is with the useful resource of a protracted manner the very first-rate body of mind for conquering demanding situations and becoming effective. It prevents you from becoming overloaded and giving up whilst confronted with a ultra-present day problem. Instead, it helps you to live centered and decided to beautify yourself.

If you need to triumph over any impediment, you need to start transferring your united states of america of thoughts from a repaired one to a growth model.

Blended State of thoughts

In the way of transferring from a hard and rapid mindset to a boom one, you may probable find out your self with a blended state of mind. A mixed frame of thoughts is one that stays in amongst a fixed and improvement one. Sometimes, you can find out yourself thinking in everyday terms, however you can discover yourself believing in growth terms at distinctive instances.

Even despite the fact which you are not wherein you want to be at the same time as you locate your self with a combined united states of america of thoughts, it is an enhancement from in the past. You need to be excited that you are making development and hold up the tough paintings. Continue to song your progress and purposefully have a development body of thoughts to step a long manner out of your set technique of thinking definitely.

Recap

When it entails limitations, perception have to make or harm you. Though it is simple to have a repaired mind-set, a improvement body of mind will assist you to overcome any obstacle and alternate it into success. Track your improvement, display a development attitude in your imaginative and prescient, and stay constructive to reveal your repaired questioning into opportunities for improvement.

Chapter 3: You're Not In Control

In addition to border of thoughts and notion, the manner you notice manage will in large element determine whether or not or now not or no longer you overcome your assignment. The influence that we're in control is broadly talking accountable for the numerous limitations we find out ourselves managing, but the barrier is illusionary.

Primarily, we should broadly diagnosed that we are not as in as lots manage as we would really like. As people, we sincerely desire control over our complete lives. Regardless of this sturdy choice to be in control, we are satisfactory in control of tremendously little.

By searching for to govern things which might be truly out of our realm of control, numerous barriers feel irritating and daunting. That's due to the reality they'll be. Seeing ourselves as on pinnacle of things creates severa fabricated barriers that we haven't any threat of getting rid of. It is essential to study this lesson if you are to overcome obstacles.

Understanding When To Let Go

Because of this control problem, some of us hang right now to barriers that we have no employer retaining onto. These might be barriers that we don't have any hazard of having rid of. Whenever we try to triumph over demanding situations that we cannot beat, we get beaten and blame ourselves. More than probably, your failure to conquer a barrier has not whatever to do with you however the truths of the problem.

With this in mind, it's miles important to go through in mind that you need to now not get caught up in matters that are not for your control. Concentrating on topics beyond your manipulate loses some time and power, and it would damage your self-esteem. Just attention on subjects that you have at the least partial manipulate over.

Whenever you discover your self dealing with a barrier which you aren't fantastic if you want to manipulate, you could desire to evaluate it. If you can't manage the barrier bring about any manner, allow circulate of it. Understanding whether or no longer you should release may be hard, but there arethings to don't forget:

1. The truths

2. Your feelings

The truths of the barrier and your emotions will decide out whether or not or not you are on top of things of the result and if you need to release it. The information of the barrier encompass anything that may be a requirement for the barrier to be triumph over.

For instance, state your challenge is that you were fired and need coins. The realities may also want to encompass the time-frame you can go along with out an earnings, the quantity of individuals relying on you, and anything else that may be objectively decided.

In addition to the facts, you need to hold in thoughts your emotions. Your feelings will commonly determine out if the project merits it to you. In some times, the venture is for your control, and the realities permit you to overcome it.

However, your feelings would probable let you know that the barrier is not clearly worth it. Let's observe an instance. Assume that your companion receives a latest process and want to skip the u . S . A .. The mission in front of you is whether or not or now not or no longer you need to glide or stay in an prolonged-time period courting.

Both of these options are possible, but, your feelings might also moreover inform you which you do not need to move and you can't tolerate an prolonged-distance dating. Because of the case, your emotions will let you recognise that this barrier isn't really nicely well worth it and that you need to in all likelihood separate.

By taking a have a observe the realities and your emotions, you need which will discern out if a barrier merits it. If the venture isn't always, offer it up and maintain collectively along with your life. Though this can take a super deal of power and energy, it will make your existence a good deal much much less hard.

How to Let Go of Control

To preserve on, you want to widely known and release manipulate. For the bulk of people, this may be tough. Here are some precious motion steps to help you launch manipulate and get yet again to dwelling a life you are taking pleasure in.

Focus on What You Can Control

The preliminary step to letting pass of manipulate is to recognition on what you could manage and recognize what you can't. What you may manipulate honestly pals with you, and the listing can be very small. Your look, mindfulness, factors of your fitness, and productivity are examples of factors which might be interior your manage.

Any scenario that consists of some other person isn't completely for your manipulate. You can manage the way you react to the alternative person, but you cannot manipulate how they act or the state of affairs.

Notice Your Response Pattern

Your response sample is the way you respond to some other man or woman or circumstance. The majority of the time, our emotions bring about our reactions. This is not lousy, but it is able to suggest which you respond badly, which harms your functionality to triumph over the assignment.

Notice your response pattern to adjust the final effects. Your response sample will consist of the cause, stress reaction, unfavourable concept, horrible feeling, reactive conduct, and the repercussion. Take a 2d to assess this response pattern so that you recognize the way you reply.

If you receive as proper with that your reaction is bad and inflicting bad results, you want to interrupt the sample. This entails gazing the trigger, respiratory, and being thoughtful to yourself and others in a few unspecified time within the future of the method.

Also, turn your terrible concept right right into a more realistic one. Changing your response sample will provide you tons greater manage over yourself. Still, it may not completely regulate the state of affairs, however, it's going to help the manner you react to it and your sensations.

Mantras

You also can use mantras to assist launch the manage freak internal you Mantras rapid and beneficial expressions that you recite to yourself in the end of the day. Studies have validated that mantras art work if you repeat them to your self often.

They alter the manner you accept as true with, and due to this, they modify the way you.

React. Here is a listing of beneficial mantras for liberating control:

• I allow circulate of the need to manipulate others.

• I release anything beyond my manipulate.

• I control myself and my happiness.

• I best manage myself and my responses.

Recap

Our need for control turns matters that we need to permit pass of into boundaries. Discover a way to find out at the same time as limitations aren't properly really worth it slow. Then, art work to permit float of your requirement to control the entirety to get again on your life and simply address obstacles that are properly really worth a while.

Chapter 4: Identifying Obstacles

Now that we have set the degree for overcoming challenges, we're capable of dig into how to show them into success. Just like some other impediment which can come collectively with your method, the initial step to conquering your barrier is to determine it. To placed it any other way, you need to apprehend what the undertaking is and classify it.

Recognizing the obstacle will make you extra privy to the positives, negatives, your very very personal biases, and what you require to do to overcome it. If you do no longer apprehend your barrier, it will possibly be now not feasible to offer you motion steps to conform with. Though there are numerous limitations, hundreds of may be labeled into larger businesses, which include managing the unknown or minimal price range.

In this chapter, we are going to check the most normal classes for stressful conditions. You might also moreover check that the obstacle in the front of you is a mixture of multiple class. That is virtually everyday. Let's take a look at what the ones everyday barrier types are.

Facing the Unknown

One of the maximum primary assignment kinds is coping with the unknown. Facing the unknown is on every occasion you find your self in a situation this is unknown territory. Whenever you go with the flow, get a logo-new venture, or communicate with a modern-day character, you can find out your self handling the unknown.

This mission can be relatively difficult for those with tension, introverted characters, and low self-self perception. That's as it takes a exquisite deal of courage and self notion to conquer this assignment and make the unknown acquainted.

The fine way to triumph over this barrier is to remind yourself that everyone has remained in a comparable state of affairs within the past, and most people are not going to determine you. Also, cope with yourself-self belief to end up more trusting of your self and your capability to act inside the unknown.

The strain to be Someone Besides Yourself

Another assignment you will in all likelihood face is strain to be a person besides your self. This stress can originate from circle of relatives, pals, or society. Some people warfare with this barrier greater than others. Ladies particularly face this undertaking, but guys do as properly.

To triumph over this obstacle, you require to apprehend in which to restoration a restrict amongst your self and others. What are your worths? What do you consider your self? What do you desire out of life? Asking these forms of problems will make clean where you finish, and one in every of a kind people begin.

To face this mission, you require to address restrict setting. As fast as you draw the road and create an excessive restriction among your self and others, you need to have the coronary heart and resolution to conform with thru. You might need to deal with your vanity and vanity to preserve the borders.

Restricted Finances

Restricted budget are a clearly hard obstacle. In numerous situations, restrained monetary sources are because of a few aspect outdoor of your control. Losing a project, welcoming a contemporary member to the own family, an unexpected mishap, and more can all bring about a minimum economic impediment.

Unlike the very lastbarriers, this one will want far more tangible and conclusive action steps. This includes producing a price variety plan, knowledge just how lots greater cash you require to make, and extra. It would possibly probably likewise need you to search for a extremely-cutting-edge way or ask for a associate to help economically.

In addition to the obvious issues that encompass restricted price range, together with not paying fees, there can also be one-of-a-kind traumatic conditions that you have to deal with, which include strained relationships, dealing with the unknown, and additional.

Relationship Issues

Relationships are a number of the maximum common locations for barriers. As human beings, we are all entitled to our mind and moves, but we regularly experience that everybody want to fall consistent with our thoughts. As a cease end result, a excellent deal of strain can be produced, and it is more tough to triumph over those stressful conditions considering that it consists of another absolutely self maintaining character.

Frequently, a barrier in a relationship is a specific event or sample. To decide the venture, you require to speak with the opportunity character to find out their side of the story. Deal with the opposite character to broaden motion steps to put off the project inside the future.

In some instances, the barrier can be irreconcilable. For example, your partner may not choice children whilst you do. Frequently, the most effective approach for overcoming this barrier is placing apart and locating a logo-new partner with the identical purpose and choice for children as you.

You also can have annoying situations associating with issues together along with your proper friends, mothers, and dads, or kids, no longer genuinely your romantic accomplice. Approach their decision inside the identical manner.

What to Do After Determining the Challenge

Once you decide the project, it's miles crucial to increase action steps which might be right now associated with the trouble to hand. Action steps offer you some factor concrete to do to overcome the barrier. Your movement steps must no longer be too lofty, but, they want to as a substitute be greater like mini-dreams.

We will speak more about this inside the next economic smash.

In addition to movement steps, you will probably require to mirror on your self. Particular boundaries will take a big toll for your highbrow and mental properly-being. Reflect on your self and awareness in your emotions. Lots of human beings are lured to location their feelings apart to put off the project suddenly.

Completely dismissing your emotions is in reality as unstable as getting swept away by way of using them. Consider your feelings and employ them as guidelines for studying. Depending on in which you stand emotionally, you may desire to speak within a self-assist e-book or see a therapist to triumph over the issues.

More instances than you will don't forget, the actual barrier lies amongst your ears, now not in the real international. Make the effort to mirror upon yourself, your desires, and your desires to come to a agency knowledge of in that you stand.

Recap

The preliminary step to overcoming the obstacle is to find out the right hassle. You can do that thru breaking apart the barrier into classifications, a good way to help the barrier to look more tangible on your mind. From there, create movement steps and call returned into your emotions to pursue a choice actively.

SET GOALS

As we referred to inside the remaining financial ruin, desires are an essential way to dispose of traumatic situations and redesign them into success. Objectives are greater tough than you may think, despite the fact that. Many people are clueless about intention development and examine-via, making it hard to triumph over boundaries.

In this bankruptcy, we're going to have a observe how you should installation desires to conquer your boundaries. These goals can be called SMART desires. Let's have a look.

SMART Objectives

The outstanding shape of targets to set is referred to as SMART desires. SMART is an acronym for precise, quantifiable, possible, realistic, and prompt. Incorporating all five of those elements into your desires makes fantastic that they'll be possible which you are able to wearing out.

A specific goal is one which has one intention in mind. It desires to be pretty focused so that you have a specific idea of what you want to advantage. More than that, the specific reason desires to be measurable. This suggests which you require so you can degree whether or not or no longer or not or now not you attained the purpose.

On pinnacle of that, it wants to be each feasible and coffee value. There is not any component in placing an purpose which you can't gain or this is sincerely out of doors of your talents. Finally, set a time frame with the resource of which you want to perform the goal. This will preserve you brought on.

For instance, say that the undertaking in the the the front of you is which you need to lessen weight. The purpose ought to be to lose 25 pounds in three months. This weight loss intention of 25 pounds specifies, quantifiable, feasible, sensible, and activate.

What If I Can't Come up With a SMART Objective?

State which you have been thinking about a SMART purpose and preserve bobbing up with now not some thing. If you find out your self in this case, you may ask a friend or relative for steerage. They can also have the ability to provide you a brand-new element of view that you hadn't considered.

If you still aren't able to give you a SMART reason, then the possibilities are that you do not have manipulate of the scenario. If you do now not have manage over it, then there is no risk to set a intention to attain it. You can set desires to relieve signs and signs and symptoms and symptoms of the barrier, however you can not assure fulfillment.

You might also stumble upon this trouble if your impediment includes another character. Say your partner desires to depart you, and you do not need a divorce. Considering that there's every one-of-a-kind similarly self maintaining person blanketed, you do no longer have complete control over the state of affairs. As a end result, you can now not have the capability to set SMART goals to make certain achievement within the state of affairs.

However, you could create SMART wants to will will let you live at the method or relate on your accomplice better. Talk via the scenario alongside side your companion to attempt to get on the same internet internet page. From there, set wants to lessen the blow. This can also furthermore contain counseling, focusing in your hobbies, or some element else that you have manage over.

Follow Through

Your dreams are nothing if you do no longer look at through with them. When you put your dreams, discover a manner to inspire yourself to maintain running at them. SMART goals are the excellent way to keep up and live recommended. Even with SMART dreams, despite the fact that, you have to maintain walking.

You might also need to create blessings for your private after breaking apart the SMART intention into smaller-sized desires or mini-goals. Every time you benefit a mini-purpose, you reward yourself. This maintains you thrilled and prepared to meet the following mini-goal.

Devote your self. Many humans set goals, but they do now not decide to them. Ensure which you take a look at through thru now not giving your self the chance to slack. Just as you'll hold someone else answerable for enjoyable their commitments, keep your self responsible moreover.

Be Flexible

When discussing dreams, we'd be amiss no longer to mention versatility. When many people set dreams, they may be very rigid and declined to flex. This is kind of a guaranteed technique to fail and now not triumph over your task. Rather, you need to be flexible, even when it relates to dreams.

Sometimes, plans trade, mission changes, or your priorities trade. When this takes place, you want to have the capacity to transport your interest and objectives to mirror this event. If no longer, the objectives can be disconnected from in that you are in lifestyles. Too stiff desires are positive to interrupt in the long run.

Instead of viewing desires as something stiff, view them as fluid. Be rigid in following thru collectively along with your goals but want to change them if you want to. Whenever the plans regulate, flexible dreams will flex with the pressure in preference to breaking.

Recap

Objectives help you accomplish your limitations. Set SMART objectives to preserve you stimulated and most likely to show your annoying situations into achievement. Though you may need to commit to your self and maintain yourself responsible, goals are simply the satisfactory approach no longer to get damaged thru your obstacles.

Chapter 5: Focus On Yourself

We can not talk about overcoming stressful situations with out discussing the importance of concentrating on ourselves and no longer comparing ourselves to others. Because of social media and lots of particular elements these days, it's miles less hard than ever to evaluate yourself to a person else.

Doing this is unfavourable to our development, fulfillment, and nicely-being. Not to mention, it makes conquering stressful conditions almost hard and locations logo-new obstacles in our lap. To triumph over limitations, you need to interrupt this habitual right away. Your complete fitness and well-being will alternate for the higher.

Though it is easy to have a look at your self to others even as handling a barrier, you want to prevent it.

Why You Shouldn't Compare Yourself to Others

The primary cause you have to no longer examine your self to others while conquering any undertaking is to supply more obstacles on the equal time. Simply located, it makes a mountain out of a molehill. If you're already forced approximately the number one obstacle, you do no longer desire to make the technique any greater hard than it desires to be.

Furthermore, comparing yourself to others may additionally additionally obstruct your capability to stay the life you preference. When you observe yourself to a person else, you are seeing yourself and them thru their thoughts-set. Doing so indicates which you are not valuing your opinions and mind as extensively as you need to.

If you continue to nicely really worth a person else's beliefs above your very private, it might be hard to overcome a barrier or produce the existence you need. Just recognition on yourself and save you evaluating yourself to others to prevent this from taking area.

Comparing Yourself to Others Develops Unrealistic Concepts

There are more than one reasons why comparing yourself is not only horrible but impractical. Most substantially, you in no way get the entire photo even as taking a examine someone from the outdoor. Individuals need to appear higher off than they're, in order that they definitely show the silver linings.

When you look at yourself to others, you're comparing your self to an unrealistic elegant. You aren't seeing the problems, boundaries, or problems they had to face to get to in which they will be. This leaves you with an unrealistic understanding of wherein you have to be.

Another motive why evaluating yourself to others is impractical is that it actually is not applicable to you. Even if you may likely get the entire photo, that you can't, it is now not your lifestyles. To make investments your power in evaluating yourself to others is a complete waste of time.

What Should You Do Rather?

Instead of evaluating yourself to others, you need to contemplate your goals and goals. This will offer you a sturdy concept approximately in that you are and in which you need to be. It is the most useful and low priced method of overcoming any impediment.

If you need to observe yourself to genuinely each person, compare your modern-day-day self for your preceding self. You need to have grown with the aid of now, and the reality you are taking numerous strive to break your relative ties exhibits which you have extra. Compare yourself on your previous self to further growth.

It is OK to speak to exceptional humans and get their guidance. Other people were through similar eventualities as you. Talk with them to find out what they're saying about the situation. Don't take their advice blindly, even though. Compare it to your thoughts and desires and skip from there.

How to Stop Comparing Yourself to Others

Here are some strategies to save you comparing yourself to others:

Know Your Triggers

Know your triggers, that are topics that make you enjoy insufficient and lead you to compare your self to others. Triggers is probably particular people on social media or stepping into particular shops. Know your triggers, so you recognize when you are probably to evaluate yourself to others.

Once you understand in which your triggers are, attempt your great to save you them. This can be tough, but, it's miles notably vital-- Unfollow folks that make you experience terrible approximately yourself or save you places that motive you to take a look at.

Remember You Don't See the Whole Story

Whenever you find out yourself slipping up, keep in thoughts which you do not see the complete story. People will placed on a the the front to make themselves seem a exquisite deal higher than they feel. Remind your self of this truth to assist carry you returned to a extra less expensive statistics.

Be Grateful for Your Life

Lastly, locate techniques to reveal greater thankfulness in your very own in your non-public existence. Look at each single trouble you want about your gift lifestyles and repeat it to your self. As you are making a listing, you will most probably find out way greater topics to love than you to start with concept.

If excessive contrast is some issue you deal with, you could desire to begin your morning or forestall your day with this idea. You will rapid find your self more thankful to your very very own lifestyles and self.

Recap

It is extremely clean to take a look at your self to others each time you're dealing with stressful situations, however you need to fight this urge. Comparing your self to others is destructive to overcoming obstacles, and it is completely impractical. Make a aware attempt to stop evaluating yourself to others to open greater fulfillment.

Chapter 6: Emotional Resilience

Whenever you deal with any problem, it's far pretty smooth to get swept away via way of your emotions and enjoy hopeless. When this takes vicinity, it is able to be subsequent to tough to eliminate the impediment at hand. One manner to neutralize those emotions is thru emotional resilience.

What is Emotional Durability?

Psychological energy is a competencies for soothing yourself every time you find out your self coping with an damaging enjoy. This negative enjoy can be your very personal emotions, a undertaking, or some thing else that reasons your mind and feelings to run widespread.

Everyone is born with a piece of intellectual power. That is how we're all naturally capable of deal with at least some hard activities. The older we get, our emotional sturdiness deepens, permitting us to deal with masses extra

difficult conditions.

You may additionally even deliberately beautify your emotional sturdiness through practices, self-compassion, and self-self warranty. Improving your intellectual resilience will permit you to get rid of any mission that comes together with your technique. It might be practical to reflect onconsideration on emotional power like a muscle. All healthful humans are born with muscles. As we broaden, our muscle tissue increase too.

Some human beings even placed inside the time to workout and aim unique muscle organizations to broaden as robust as viable. Whenever we find out ourselves required to reinforce a few problem or provoke a probable date, we would flex our muscle businesses. To positioned it definitely, we appoint our muscles all the time, but we are able to bend them every time we choice.

Our emotional resilience is the equal manner. Psychological durability assists us at a few stage in the day, but, it is able to be preferred greater so within the route of person activities.

How Does Emotional Resilience Assist You Overcome Barriers?

Psychological resilience is vital for now not truely conquering limitations but converting them into fulfillment. It is only via intellectual electricity that we experience we are able to address problems and decorate on our existence. This is an essential element of having rid of limitations that you cannot forget about about.

Let's take into account a lifestyles in that you had no intellectual resilience. You also can rapidly give up, cry, and get down on yourself because of the barrier. You aren't able to manage your mind or feelings, inhibiting you from putting off the impediment.

However, with emotional power, you may be able to non violent your thoughts and rationally talk to your self. This capacity should then will assist you to recollect rational strategies for conquering the obstacle to alternate it into achievement.

Aspects of Emotional Durability

The great detail about emotional resilience is that you may boom it. Whether you are very mentally resistant or not, you may constantly find out a piece extra. In well-known, emotional resilience consists of 3 factors: the bodily components, mental factors, and social components. You should popularity on all additives to improve your psychological resilience.

Physical factors encompass your energy, health, and power. If you're ill and your frame might no longer artwork as it want to, it is lots tougher to be mentally resilient. If you do now not presently, attention on ingesting extremely good nutritious food and getting a few exercise to assist enhance your emotional strength.

The intellectual factors embody your self-self warranty, vanity, adjustability, emotional recognition, attention, self-expression, and reasoning capabilities. These factors are critical to having applicable emotional resilience. You might require to do a number of person art work to aim this element, relying in your particular requirements.

For example, you may probably have a hassle with self-self belief but be extremely good to your reasoning capabilities. If that is the case, you may need to visit a therapist to talk via the reasons that you are feeling adversely approximately your self. Other human beings also can moreover have the opportunity trouble. They might also moreover have fantastic shallowness but low thinking abilties. Those people may moreover preference to start locating out more to undertaking their brains.

Finally, the 0.33 aspect is social additives. This is your interpersonal relationships, interaction abilities, and cooperation. Human beings are not created to be lone creatures. Boost your intellectual resilience via deepening your connections and conversation skills with others. They can be discovered beneficial every time you cope with an obstacle.

Structure Psychological Strength

Whenever you need to bring together your mental durability, it's far top notch to solve the 3 additives above. Some people might also moreover need beneficial aid with the relationship element however be remarkable with the opportunity two. Reflect on yourself to observe which factors you may need to decorate. The majority of humans want to decorate all three to some diploma.

From there, you need to be watchful about your mind and moves. Notification each time you experience terrible approximately your self or whenever you sense which include you lose control. As you are noticing your thoughts and movements, exercise talking your self down and self-compassion.

Talking your self down includes unwinding your thoughts. See if there are any contradictions or logical factors which are available on your mind. Unmasking the ones mind will will can help you come to plenty extra degree-minded region. In addition to specializing in your self, take the time to deepen your relationships. This is probably as clean as installing a lunch collectively with your mothers and pa, but it would additionally be as high-quality as soliciting for help from a friend.

You would possibly even want to speak approximately what you've got been locating in your project for self-reflected photograph even as deepening your social relationships. If you are locating constructing your mental durability to be as an alternative tough, recollect talking to a therapist or certified expert. These experts will help making a decision your trouble mind and unwind them to boom your emotional sturdiness.

Recap

Psychological resilience is critical to overcome any barrier. Much like a muscle, your intellectual strength can be grown through deliberate mind and actions. Even in case you are presently emotionally resilient, preserve to develop this muscle to assist redecorate any barrier into fulfillment.

Chapter 7: Turn Challenges Into Success

Lastly, we've were given reached the ultimate financial ruin of this e-book. Up till now, we have spoken approximately the fact approximately limitations and the manner belief and the faux illusion of manage in particular decide your capability to triumph over them. We've likewise mentioned figuring out limitations, placing desires, concentrated on yourself, and emotional energy that will help you discover a way through your challenge.

But how do you rework a project into fulfillment? After all, truely overcoming the task is not like prospering. In this financial disaster, we're going to offer you with critical mind now not really to overcome your barrier however trade it into an effective image of fulfillment in your existence.

Practice, Practice, Practice

As the antique preserving goes, practice makes perfect. To beat any task that comes your manner, you have to have workout in conquering them. This suggests that transforming obstacles into success is probably hard initially, but it'll get a whole lot easier as you circulate. This is a herbal truth about lifestyles.

Practice all of the hints above each time you face a venture, irrespective of how small the obstacle may also seem. Consider this as barrier energy schooling. This training will help you get into the exercise of getting rid of barriers to finding out exactly what you want to cope with inner yourself.

If you don't feel like you've got got any boundaries to exercise on, you probably aren't looking difficult sufficient. Obstacles are so common in our existence that almost all of them cross undetected. Take a vital take a look at your every day life, and you may possibly find out a challenge orconcealing there.

Don't Quit

Some annoying conditions can be greater tough than others. Make certain no longer to surrender. Even if you experience stuck and just like the technique isn't always working, preserve popularity employer. Only via non-stop attempt are you able to transform demanding situations into success. Of route, this is not much like letting move while it is now not nicely really worth it. If your gut is telling you which you must not be disturbing masses over a powerful issue, then be privy to it.

But do not cease in reality because of the truth the problem is difficult, or you are concerned. Giving up out of fear will simplest damage you. Plus, you may in all likelihood regret it within the future, and existence's too brief to regret any actions!

Stay Optimistic

One of the very extraordinary strategies to make certain that you do no longer quit is to live exquisite. As we already said, there may be continuously no less than one brilliant to any impediment you face. Keep those favorable for your thoughts's eye to stay fine.

In addition to final high-quality approximately the stressful conditions you cope with, live best approximately your self too. If you feel that you cope with self-self belief or self-respect, talk on your doctor. These are surprisingly crucial worries that require to be resolved.

Stay exceptional approximately your life as an entire too. Even if you are not precisely in which you want to be however, widely known that you are within the direction of conducting your aim than ever in advance than. This will can help you stay thrilled about going via your disturbing situations given which you are already so near your give up intention.

You're Not In The Clear Yet

As soon as you triumph over the barrier handy, it is probably tempting to respire a sigh of treatment and don't forget you're in the clean. Though you need to virtually commemorate and get excited about conquering your barrier, you aren't within the smooth however.

As we have were given stated on occasion at some stage in this e-book, barriers are throughout. Even if you triumph over one does not advocate that it's miles going to be clean cruising from proper proper here on out. Soon, every different impediment will come your manner.

Be prepared for upcoming barriers through persevering with to push yourself, even at the same time as you do not revel in find it irresistible. This may want to in all likelihood appear excessive, however this continual pursuit of improvement is what will redecorate your limitations into fulfillment. Focus on your self and your enhancement, even though the task is over.

Recap

The best way to convert a task into fulfillment is to mix what you have were given obtained from this e book into your every day existence. While you face a challenge and overcome it, hold to exercise and push yourself to make use of the ones techniques. Just then will you word a actual change internally, so that you can let you be triumphant some place else on your life?

Chapter 8: Why Don't We Have Enough Self-Discipline?

This question has plagued humankind for decades now. Ever for the reason that we've got existed in this earth, one has to marvel why some people actually do no longer have the sector or the pressure to push via to what they want to do in lifestyles. When in fact, it is easy to advantage a wonderful experience of order in a unmarried's existence even as not having to exert an excessive amount of strive. What leads to an undisciplined life for maximum human beings? How do we save you this from ever affecting our lives negatively? These are absolutely a number of the questions that this monetary smash interests to reply.

Discipline vs. Distractions

The important enemy of manipulate is a distraction. A distraction, in the truest revel in of the word, is defined as some factor that diverts the eye of an character. Anything that locations someone out of focus may be considered a distraction (for example, searching television in preference to cooking dinner or playing outdoor in region of doing all your homework).

While some of those sports are not dangerous on their private, doing them in greater can divert your interest from doing extra critical subjects on your life. The factor is, if you need to reap concern, you may want to discover ways to reputation all of your interest on one efficient pastime that let you enhance now not most effective yourself, but others as properly. If you want to accumulate your goal, you need to learn how to grow to be greater invested in self-improvement and not allow some thing else seize your hobby. At least not until you advantage your reason.

Various Types of Distractions

To give you a clearer picture of the manner distractions can negatively have an impact in your quest for discipline, proper right here are some brilliant kinds of amusement. We may even show you a few specific examples of the way distractions can harm your disciplinary normal.

Physical Distractions

Have you ever felt stricken with the resource of the affiliation of your furniture? Have you ever idea about exercising, but constantly generally tend to area it off because of work? These are clearly a number of the primary examples of physical distractions. A bodily distraction can be described as a tangible item or fabric that would physically hinder you from doing what you want to do.

In this case, the litter on your mattress room or the physical appearance of your residing room can divert your interest in this sort of manner which you may as a substitute do some aspect else and not address the situation on hand in any respect. One reason inside the lower again of this educate of idea is probably pressure. If you enjoy careworn approximately physical pastime or exerting an excessive amount of effort, opportunities are you'll do the whole thing to your power to keep away from it. This aversion is what brings me to the second one form of distraction: The Mental Distraction.

The Mental Distraction

Sometimes, the best obstacles to concern are our mind. We are consequences distracted via some thing that might entice our interest and weaken our awareness. For instance, in choice to workout, we might rather spend our time sitting in the the front of the pc playing video video video games or on foot on important files for our challenge. While the ones activities may be useful in special additives of our lives, doing this in more can be detrimental to our physical health in the end. This fitness danger is why it's miles essential for us to acquire balance as lots as feasible.

Additionally, if an man or woman has a hassle that he can not seem to find out a solution for, a few people select to cognizance their electricity on seeking out to remedy the problem first in advance than doing something else. If this takes place, he or she can become neglecting other factors of their life. As an example, I will provide you with a situation:

Maria wants to lose weight however has too many stuff on her plate proper now. From the desires of her workplace paintings to the pressure delivered about through her own family and personal lifestyles, she honestly does not have the time to do some aspect physical to beautify herself. Hence, she ended up gaining many kilos, which ultimately took a toll on her arrogance.

The wishes of her paintings lifestyles and private existence constitute the two varieties of distraction in her life, inflicting her to participate in each day sports that seem harmless enough, however these severa sports activities have turn out to be destructive often because of the gradual and steady buildup that ultimately rendered her not capable of do something else for herself.

The Emotional Distractions

Emotional distractions can represent a apparently clean but complicated form of diversion. For me, this is the hardest sort of distraction to address due to the reality you are contending together together with your very private emotions. An emotionally distracted individual may be at risk of perception and first-rate interest-grabbing sports that might not be properly for their fitness. As an example, I will use the quite dangerous nature of emotional consuming.

Emotional eating may be defined due to the fact the act of using meals as a way to break out emotional distress. The deed can bring about immoderate weight gain and occasional conceitedness. How does it relate to energy of will or the dearth thereof? Let me supply an motive behind. If an character lets his feelings dictate whilst he eats, it's far specially possibly that he has no manage over this precise impulse in his existence. This action suggests at the character of the character. It method that he we ought to himself end up so emotionally beaten that he feels trapped in the first-rate manner to break out might be to stuff himself to divert his mind.

By doing this, he defeats the cause of energy of will as a whole. It virtually is going to reveal that he isn't on pinnacle of factors of his feelings and impulses, that is why it might be vital to take him out of the state of affairs and assist him recognize the reasons inside the lower back of his moves. Once he can figure out the terrible motivations that push him to deal with his problems in this kind of negligent manner, he can then pursue a lifestyles of power of mind.

In precis, the primary reason we are not capable of reap electricity of mind as an entire is due to the shortage of hobby and actual motivation. Once an character can discover the proper motivation for becoming a accountable man or woman who is on top of factors of his feelings and actions, he or she is probably capable of obtain the motive of becoming a self-actualized character who will no longer allow some thing or every person dictate how he need to live his lifestyles. He will then have whole autonomy of his moves and be able to do some thing he desires to do with out sacrificing his fitness inside the way.

Chapter 9: Ways By Which Self-Discipline Can Transform Our Lives

A alternate in manner of lifestyles can offer you with what you want concerning transformation and new beginnings. This being said, you have to have a certain revel in of control over your life an excellent way to flow approximately correctly making adjustments. You can simplest reap this control with the useful resource of ensuring which you have sufficient field to your device so you can be a part of the adjustments which you want to arise in your existence and keep them because of this.

In this financial disaster, we are in a position to speak the severa special techniques that strength of thoughts can genuinely trade our lives for the better. I choice that when analyzing this monetary disaster, you may be able to see how you can successfully alternate your lifestyle to reflect a whole new mind-set about the subjects that you need to do for your lifestyles. Here are a number of the specific strategies through which energy of will can assist regulate the course of your route within the days to return returned.

A New Beginning

Whether you need to look at a brand new talent or exchange the way you appearance, beginning something new requires fidelity and exercising. You want to do some thing time and again to educate your body a manner to circulate in a way that would supplement the brand new capability that you need to adopt. The identical is going for beginning a modern dependancy. If you want to start ingesting vegetables, it's going to now not be easy due to the fact within the beginning, of course, your frame will must regulate to the new components of the ingested remember.

This exchange is why you want to have fidelity on your existence. You want to introduce wonderful additives of your new life into your device in order that your body received't skip into marvel. Self-Discipline enters the image when you have to maintain your new way of existence. It will now not be smooth.

For instance, maintaining your pleasant weight isn't always clean on the same time as you're commonly surrounded thru scrumptious food. However, if you are sufficiently targeted and you've got sufficient motivation to preserve your weight, you may do the entirety on your strength to preserve it off.

Likewise, if you want to study a state-of-the-art capability, everyday practice is critical. Athletes have a tendency to spend hours in the fitness center actually to exercising frequently and exercising their hobby. They also need to preserve a healthy weight loss plan and lease a few modifications in their manner of life so one can hone their competencies and keep them as sharp as feasible. Ultimately, what I am pronouncing is which you want to paintings hard for what you need to advantage. Having strength of will will assist you do clearly that and in addition.

Self-Discipline Can Help Change Points of View

Self-field will permit you to change your mind-set. If you have got trouble, you could have no purpose to make excuses approximately what you have to do approximately your numerous self-development goals. Making excuses is in the end detrimental to self-development. If you are usually making excuses approximately what you have to do or what you want to no longer do, you becomes no longer being able to do a little aspect the least bit. Sometimes, you certainly must take motion and do something advantageous approximately your state of affairs.

For instance, if you want to get out of the residence but then feel like you may't because of the reality you would certainly end up bumping into someone unsavory, possibilities are you could simply emerge as making excuses about having an excessive amount of housekeeping to do or being too worn-out to exit.

However, when you have subject, you'll end up developing a time desk of your chores and the severa other things which you need to do within the residence. You will adhere and stick with this system regardless of what takes vicinity. Discipline in its truest essence refers to being able to begin some component and give up it surely, without criticism.

Self-Discipline Can Help You Become Goal-Oriented

If you need to attain your desires, you could do the entirety to your power to get what you need. Self-area is the answer. Being able to art work difficult to get what you want. There's not anything more pleasurable than information which you have worked hard for a few issue that you've earned.

For example, in case you need to have washboard abs, you need to spend a whole lot of time in the gymnasium to artwork in your abdominal muscle groups. Exercising takes self-discipline and passion. Subsequently, in case you don't have place, you could never be able to attain your intention effectively.

Giving Yourself a Deadline

Having a hint strain for your lifestyles can get your juices flowing. It is all part of turning into goal-orientated because of energy of will as nicely. Some human beings declare to art work nicely underneath pressure. This idea is simple to apprehend due to the truth at the same time as you are below strain, you have not any preference but to supply outcomes after a positive prescribed length. Having energy of will will let you reap your intention of accomplishing this ultimate date as short as viable.

Discipline and Focus

In connection with having a time restriction, you may be capable of gather your reduce-off date in case you are centered enough on what you have to do. Let us say that you are an athlete who desires to be in pinnacle form for a scheduled in form in six months. Because of the time constraint, you'll have no choice however to artwork difficult to be organized in time for the event. To effectively do this, you need to interest on enhancing your physical body further on your mind. You will need to learn how to forget about about all your troubles and emotional apprehensions about the sport. All you can do now can be focus on schooling your craft to hone it so you can win.

This specific concept points to having general consciousness. With interest, you will be capable of reflect onconsideration on one intention and one reason on my own. There are many strategies by using the use of which you can collect focus. However, we are in a position to talk about it in the next few chapters.

Self-Discipline Teaches About Responsibility

Having energy of will way being accountable for your actions. If you're on pinnacle of things of your behavior and mind, possibilities are you gained't do a little element to damage others or damage yourself within the technique. Discipline is all about control. It is the capability to no longer succumb for your primary instincts. If you could do that, you'll turn out to be a responsible citizen for fine.

Chapter 10: Building The Self-Confidence

A proper hero is defined via strength of will. I say this not truly due to the fact soldiers are required to have the frame and capability essential for doing battle. I say this due to the fact warriors are recognized to have a code that they're certain to put into effect, now not most effective on themselves but their fellow infantrymen as nicely.

The Confidence of a True Warrior

According to the fighter's code, a warrior can not in reality be considered someone who fights. Neither can a fighter be described as a person who prepares for struggle and fights the warfare. A actual hero is a person who has specific more noble requirements aside from his or her physical prowess. He need to be type and considerate. Being a warrior, he's going to now not have a hassle setting the desires of others in advance than his personal. He is confident sufficient in himself that he does not with out trouble get jealous of various humans's success.

A Warrior Fights to Protect Others

A warrior isn't always afraid to go into conflict for each person who cannot protect themselves. They do not display off their bodily energy and capability simply to electrify exceptional people. They use their strength to assist out folks that are in want. If you need to be a real warrior, you need to be inclined to be of carrier to others.

A Warrior Will Never Start A Fight

A actual warrior need to in no way start bodily brawls. However, he ought to also now not be afraid to finish one. A warrior is aware about his power and as plenty as feasible could now not need to trouble others to the pain that he can reason. Various martial arts specialists within the route of statistics live through the usage of this code. Additionally, a real warrior will not fight a person who can't defend themselves.

Soldiers in battle similarly to ancient Greek and Roman gladiators commonly made it a issue to fight someone whom they considered same. Similarly constructed ladies and men who could be capable of guard themselves, if crucial.

A Warrior Always Tries to Do the Honorable Thing

A actual warrior is described through manner of being honorable. For instance, heroes like King David or Joan of Arc and Lapu-Lapu fought one among a type conquerors who preferred to take their land. They fought for what they believed in and bought. They did not do it for the distinction or the recognition. They honestly did it as it became the proper element to do. This concept additionally applies to healthful people who need to be disciplined and live useful lives.

A Warrior's Only Enemy Is Himself

A proper warrior does now not spend his days fretting over defeat. Instead, he spends it enhancing his competencies even in addition. If, as an instance, you meet someone who's higher than you at a few factor, it might no longer be green to gripe over not triumphing. Instead, you have to study from the enjoy and strive not to commit the equal errors once more. This way, if ever you do stumble upon the same state of affairs or the equal people, you'll end up because the victor for certain. Discretion is the manner you certainly improve your self and turn out to be better than you have been earlier than.

If you need to have a warrior's self warranty, continuously endure in thoughts the tenets noted above. This way, you may be capable of stay your life in step with proper values that turns into the stuff of legends in future years. Allow them to guide you down the proper direction to self-discovery and electricity. I am wonderful that you'll in no way bypass incorrect in case you use the ones tenets.

Real self notion is defined with the aid of the use of using the functionality to discover humility in your understanding. It is the functionality to use your God-given talents to make one of a type human beings's lives higher. If you could try this, you can take solace in the truth that the sector is probably a higher place with you round.

Chapter 11: Gaining The Motivation Of A Spartan

The Famous Story Of The Spartans

One critical element of strength of thoughts is motivation. A man or woman desires to be sufficiently stimulated to act undoubtedly. This factor is why you want to advantage as an awful lot motivation as you may to collect your desires.

In this monetary catastrophe, we can can help you know the tale of the Spartans and the way they have become the mythical warriors they had been in historic Greece.

The Story of Spartans

According to Greek facts, the Spartan army have come to be composed of males and females who've been professional within the art work of army conflict from infancy as a good deal as adulthood. Because of this, the race have become the maximum famous and most effective warriors that ever lived. As stated in advance, Spartan males and females are expert in all styles of fight. The army adopts a military-fashion training regimen as well. However, Spartan children are also knowledgeable in severa fields like song, arts, or even politics. This shape of schooling turns them into the maximum nicely rounded human beings that might ever exist on this earth.

Training from Infancy

Spartan recruitment begins at infancy. As quickly as a Spartan toddler is born, each is inspected for any deformities and weaknesses. The Spartan Council of Elder or Gerousia does the inspection. If the child is deemed risky, he's left to die in the mountains. However, a few historians contested that the exercising of leaving the weakest offspring in the mountains to die changed into in standard completed in Athens, Greece.

The Spartan Wisdom and Way of Life

The Gerousia agree with that babies who were prone and deformed had no place in Sparta. Children are knowledgeable on the age of 7 to end up the maximum formidable males and females that could ever exist. Historians constantly say that one Spartan warrior is same to masses of infantrymen and warriors from particular Grecian islands.

While this might be an exaggeration, it bodes well for placing fear in opposition to Spartan enemies of the country. Once you live in Sparta, you'll be appeared to your prowess in battle. According to legend, Spartans are willed and dedicated warriors who will never back off from a fight or give up willingly.

The Spartans live via a code of honor that is strictly enforced. They agree with that all men are created equal and that equality particularly matters want to be included in any respect fees. These are great tenets to live thru for positive.

This code is why it might be awesome if you can adopt certain elements of the Spartan manner of living. Mainly how they devise themselves with self perception even beneath pressure. To achieve this stage of remember and vicinity, you need to undergo rigorous education like they did. In the subsequent few chapters, you could find out truly what form of training it takes to become the maximum disciplined and sturdy-willed individual that you can ever be.

Spartan Training and Its Benefits

What is taken into consideration considered one of a kind about Spartan army training is that it begins at such an early age that you will be able to stay and breathe the doctrine as quick as you begin.

Spartan kids develop as lots as study through the most fearsome warriors the area has ever stated. They are taught quite a few topics from sports activities and military techniques to immoderate art work of survival and army battle.

Because of this, they will be pushed with the useful resource of the trap of combat. Being a Spartan warrior approach that you'll be capable of do anything it takes to stay on. As they are saying, Spartans have emerge as synonymous with fearlessness, cruelty, and staying strength. Apart from being warriors, they stay clean lives and need now not some thing.

This form of high motivation and easy dwelling can instill vicinity in an person. This archaic exercise also can be in assessment to that of army schooling. Yes, it is probably inundated, but it is also noticeably beneficial regarding turning someone so shy into the most succesful person. With this kind of education, you could not must worry about now not being capable of do something that you need on your lifestyles. You will method to no character and feature the electricity to guide your self and your family as nicely.

In brief, this is the form of motivation that you want to undertake in case you want to come to be self-assured and disciplined in each element of your existence. I am sure that you may now not regret gift system this type of entire of existence training to enhance your self appreciably.

Therefore, if you need to become the right definition of trouble and power, one trouble is for sure: you need to paintings tough for it. It will not be smooth. You want to spend your days thinking about how it may help others in case you emerge as the maximum capable man or woman you can be.

While Spartans had been motivated through combat and the advantage of bodily power, they were also diagnosed to uphold an honorable code that became the cause for his or her braveness and ferocity in struggle. To be capable of shield distinct human beings and their land from conquerors who might need to take it faraway from them. This shape of motivation offers them cognizance and the pressure to teach even extra difficult.

Finding Your Motivation

If you want to collect a wonderful degree of vicinity, it's miles crucial that you can inspire yourself to paintings hard. This motivation is difficult to discover, especially for self-development obligations. If this is your hassle, then it would be useful so you can discover the proper form of motivation that could beneficial useful resource you to stay heading in the proper course.

In this phase, we are capable of try to give you a few pointers on a way to inspire your self to benefit the best stage of electricity of mind which you want to gain lifestyles.

Finding Your Center

The first element that you need to do is live silent. Listen to what your heart tells you to do. Ask your self a few questions earlier than you begin your schooling. Why are you doing this? Is it to beautify your self physical? To make you experience higher approximately yourself? Whatever your purpose can be, it has to have enough weight to hold you through positive painful episodes within the education.

Sometimes, people who go through a energetic education consultation to beautify themselves normally have a propensity to stop within the course of the early degrees because of the ache and physical struggling that most of them ought to undergo. The vigorousness of schooling is why you need to have a smooth motivation. You will now not advantage location until you are committed on your reason. You can most effective try this in case you are properly inspired.

Below are a number of the suitable motivators that any character can also moreover have and use for his or her schooling.

Health

Keeping yourself healthy is one of the best motivations that you may have for self-development. However, it can be tough to benefit a wholesome body without self-control. You want to be definitely committed on your reason.

Family

You additionally can be inspired to higher your self with the assist of your own family. This manner, you could have all of the help which you need to move on on every occasion you begin falling off the wagon of problem. Your own family can assist placed you once more on path each time you sense like preventing your exercise recurring or in case you enjoy like dishonest in your weight loss plan. Whatever the cause can be, having circle of relatives around is a incredible detail for assist.

Emotions

Are you irritated about a few component? Would you want to take revenge on every person who has wronged you? These two examples reflect terrible feelings as a cause. However, it may trade into advantageous reinforcement concerning your bodily transformation. As a race, Spartans lived a military sort of lifestyle, they have been driven through the belief of defeating the enemy in war. Winning is in truth a super using force for a person to enhance themselves. So if you need to become the most disciplined man or woman, you need to study to reveal into a bit of a Spartan -- a robust warrior driven through his motivation to fight.

Fight on your proper to stay, combat to protect your family, but most of all, combat for yourself and a better lifestyles inside the future.

Chapter 12: Learning To Focus

Doing It Like A Navy Seal

Being capable of hobby is one of the maximum important tendencies which you want to increase if you want to emerge as self-disciplined. This segment may be able that will help you discover how navy employees (in particular navy seals) are taught to recognition at some point of their schooling. I am positive that you'll no longer remorse studying this element because of the fact you'll examine masses about the military and the way they increase their squaddies to emerge as the maximum elite business enterprise of fighters and protectors round the world.

The Significance of Military Training

In the navy, soldiers are taught and professional to grow to be each physical and mentally organized for struggle. Learning these precious training is why it is probably great for every person to enlist in the navy if handiest to get the schooling that they offer.

With this bodily training, you'll be able to growth amazing fight talents in addition to gain entire highbrow control with a purpose to be pleasant in all factors of your life. This phase will provide an explanation for how navy education precise best to the ones of army seals assist you to attain notable cognizance and highbrow alertness.

The Advantage of Goal Setting

Initially, what you need to do is ensure that you could set dreams for yourself. In army seal education, it's been positioned out via military scientists that the most successful trainees are human beings who have been able to set short-time period dreams for themselves.

Through studies, specialists determined out that those trainees have been able to stay on via way of ensuring that they'll be capable of focus at the assignment. The critical thoughts of these people targeted on completing what they must do now. They do no longer waste their time considering what to do subsequent.

By doing this, they're able to get through the subsequent short while of the challenge and do the subsequent sports without delay. If you need to have a look at more approximately aim placing, the subsequent bankruptcy will speak it in entire.

Mental Visualization

Navy seals have been capable of cognizance more on their education thru the use of the art of highbrow visualization. Whenever they're resting, they reflect onconsideration on what they really would like to do as opposed to schooling. For example, in area of training, a military seal can also additionally want to move swimming at the beach or be aware about tune. By doing this, they may attention and raise themselves up from the problems that they're experiencing throughout training. It is likewise extraordinarily beneficial to make use of it at some stage in traumatic situations. Instead of an emphasis at the strain, take into account something effective. Something so as to raise your spirits up and make you overlook the difficulty and physical stress of the task handy.

Positive Self-Talk

Navy seals can live to inform the tale disturbing conditions because of the fact they're in a position to talk themselves into believing that a few thing well will come out of their schooling. As they're pronouncing, tough instances don't last, tough human beings do. If you need to attain awareness, you need to apprehend that the whole thing ought to have an surrender in the long run. Something precise will pop out of your situation, and you virtually need to see it via.

Deep Breathing Techniques

Lastly, you need to discover ways to manipulate your physical tics. Most of the time, strain can carry out the worst in human beings, each mentally and physical. In a number of the ones times, the human beings that display signs and symptoms and signs and signs and symptoms of being overwhelmed display up bodily movements and special changes that may be seen overtly. Due to worry, they are able to begin to have bloodless and clammy arms. These are in reality some of the physical signs of stress that maximum human beings can experience. However, you may control these through the use of the navy seal method of deep breathing.

Just take a deep breath and hold it in for 4-seconds and exhale for approximately a four-2nd remember quantity as well. Deep breathing physical games will assist relax and deliver oxygen to the mind right now. If enough oxygen is furnished to the mind, your body might be able to loosen up greater, for that reason putting off your physical tics.

These are actually some of the diverse techniques at the way to learn how to attention on military seal schooling. I can assure you that those steps can be the most inexperienced you could ever find concerning venture a greater sense of interest and subject in the end.

Chapter 13: Setting Goals And How To Stick To Them

In the previous bankruptcy, we targeted on some of the techniques that lets in you to learn how to recognition. One of those numerous methods is to set desires for your self. In this financial catastrophe, we are able to find out how you may do this while not having to go returned to vintage forms of behavior.

We will give you some hints on how you could have a control way of lifestyles changes so as not to weigh down you when they rise up. If you want to start placing dreams for your self and circulate further down the path to finish power of will, I suggest that you look at without delay to observe extra.

Simplify

The first element which you want to do is simplify. Set a few smaller desires so that you can acquire initially. For instance, in case you need to shed pounds, your last intention should be to maintain the weight off. But you can't do this in case you don't begin someplace, right?

You can begin via ingesting smaller food each day. Eating smaller portions of food will allow your frame to modify to the slight modifications to your diet plan. You don't must starve your self. What you want to do is to reduce down at the quantities of your food and in the end your body will now not crave as plenty meals anymore.

Do a Little Bit More Every Day

Secondly, what you need to do is permit your body modify to your sports activities which might be greater physical. Staying targeted on the weight loss goal may be difficult. However, if you take it sluggish and sluggish, you will be capable of collect what you need with out lovely your device notably. Try to do some bit greater bodily interest every day. For example, why don't you walk throughout the house for 15 minutes every day? Then after your frame receives used to transferring round in shorter intervals of time, make a factor to boom the period. The key here is to permit your frame modify to the smaller adjustments in advance than you waft massive.

The number one reason people end up going once more to their antique behavior is that their body is in denial. It modified into so used to the way it have become in advance than you changed a while desk that any slight adjustments inside the ordinary might also need to have destructive results on your physical form.

To cope with this, you need to make the exchange sluggish. Eventually, you will find out that your body isn't aching to move decrease lower returned to the way it turned into anymore.

The equal principle applies at the same time as you are attempting to wean your self off a selected form of interest or food. It doesn't help to move cold turkey. You must take it sluggish to ensure more achievement.

Start With the Easiest Task

Another manner an exceptional way to gain purpose setting is to make certain that you may do smooth duties. The cause your body refuses to be simply right for you is that it unearths it hard to do the task on hand. If you have got many desires set and masses of things to do, begin with a few aspect easy then paintings your manner to the harder ones.

For example, if the remaining intention for you is to be more assertive, the exceptional way as a manner to accumulate this purpose is to make certain that you assert your self whilst making small alternatives. Assert yourself at the equal time as you're trying to decide what to place on. When doing this, attempt to keep away from inquiring for different human beings's critiques. Focus on what YOU need to place on.

The key right here is to make sure that you may keep in mind your desires first in advance than genuinely everyone else's. If you could decide on the little things without a problem, you'll discover that it'll not be hard a very good manner to make massive choices ultimately.

Ultimately, what you want to do with motive placing is to make sure that you could begin someplace sincere. Having a clear plan will make your goals remaining longer due to the fact they do not seem too hard. You may be able to preserve the situations of the purpose give up end result effortlessly due to the fact you damage it down into clean duties.

Classify Your Goals

It would possibly help to break up your desires into booths. You can write a checklist for your brief-time period and long-time period desires. You need to do this so that you may want to have a clean intellectual picture of what you need to be doing collectively together with your lifestyles.

Here is every different instance: in case you want to tour but find it hard to do it due to extremely good duties that you want to hold, the excellent way in case you need to acquire the cause is to set aside time to journey brief distances. Going to shut by way of places will put together you in your intention of journeying the area ultimately.

Because of your normal touring to locations nearby, you may be able to discover what you need to want to journey remote places. Think of it as an remarkable manner to research. You will genuinely experience yourself as properly.

The Significance of Motivation in Goal Setting

Additionally, your motivation for carrying out your cause is also critical. Why do you want to excursion? Why do you need to shed pounds? You want to introspect and make certain that your motivations for placing the ones dreams are well worth it. Otherwise, you can become reverting on your antique behavior.

In precis, what I am attempting to mention is that during motive setting, it does no longer depend variety variety how smooth or menial the intention is. The important factor is that you can start doing some issue approximately getting what you need. As they say, a adventure of 1 thousand miles begins with a unmarried step.

Chapter 14: Turning Decisions Into Habits, And Habits Into Behavior, And Behavior Into Success

Definite selection-making is an critical part of willpower. It permits you to move ahead collectively together with your quest to turn out to be better as a person and a effective member of the community. In this bankruptcy, we are able to speak how you can research the artwork of desire-making and flip it into a few factor behavioral.

How to Make It a Habit

Developing the dependancy of making a decision is some component that can be specially tough to do if you are used to developing picks your self. It can be very daunting for some humans because of the truth it's miles a exceptional duty and burden to preserve. However, this financial catastrophe will display you that you simply need to infuse choice-making into your personal subculture with the aid of the usage of following those easy steps.

Take Risks from Time to Time

The proper trouble about placing smaller dreams for yourself is that you may be capable of make the apparently unimportant alternatives at the manner to not have any large ramifications on your existence. For instance, if you want to devour some element, the choice to select amongst cake and ice cream may be simpler. You do no longer even want to take into account it. Using impulsive wondering will allow you to exercise short wondering.

Quick questioning is the primary key to living a a success lifestyles. You do not want to reflect onconsideration on your preference too much, specially even as subjected to strain or strain. If you exercise it lengthy enough, you may be capable of take calculated risks extra often. Always keep in thoughts that there can be time for contemplation, and there may be time for motion as properly. Do now not waste it sluggish thinking about what you have to do at the same time as you already understand the answer on your query.

Learn How to Simplify

That being said, you can't "wing it" all of the time, in particular even as making crucial selections. There are various factors to preserve in mind whilst you decide. These severa problems are the reasons why you have to begin small. This way, you could get used to searching at situations in a miles much less complicated mind-set. Once you learn how to simplify, making the large alternatives may be less complicated in the end.

Consider All the Facts

Personally speaking, as quickly as I try and determine what to do with a specific scenario in my lifestyles, I continuously try to reflect onconsideration on it as a math hassle. I bear in mind the given facts of the case first. Then I create a digital equation the use of the given variables that I truely have on the table. Think of it as doing all your homework. If you are attempting to determine whether or not or not or now not to do it nowadays or day after today, just rent the problem-solving techniques. Considering the given information, what ought to take region in case you cast off doing all your homework? When is the closing date for the artwork?

Only Make a Decision after Considering All the Facts

Once you've got were given had been given effectively gathered all the critical information that could assist you decide what to do about your trouble, make a preference. Avoid taking a half of of-baked route of movement as a top notch deal as you can. This will motive much less hassle. By being massive approximately it, it will make you extra confident approximately any choice that you plan to make within the future.

One of the primary motives why human beings 2d-bet themselves is due to the fact they didn't expect matters through. Acting on impulse will hone your talents in taking motion on the same time as deliberating approximately lifestyles can offer you with the opportunity to evaluate the situation. Finding the proper stability a few of thecan be hard, however if you are going to exercising continuously, the whole lot will ultimately fall into region for you.

To encapsulate this financial disaster, one crucial element which you need to take into account even as making decisions is that you have to be prepared. Learn all that you could approximately the state of affairs handy and simplify. Making matters as smooth as feasible will allow you to make sound alternatives with out even exerting too much strive.

Chapter 15: 20 Traits Of Successful People

This section will focus on 20 character trends that a fulfillment people own. It will offer you with an idea of what it takes to come to be excellent in every undertaking that you select to do to your lifestyles. I choice that you'll be able to develop those dispositions your self or in the end find out which you had they all alongside.

1. Fearlessness

Successful people don't have any fear. They are not afraid to take risks and are prepared to face the consequences of their actions.

2. Decisiveness

Successful human beings can make sound options on their non-public without leaving any stone unturned. They can have a look at severa quantities of facts at the same time as not having a bias. They can decide on the same time as now not having doubts.

3. No Retreat, No Surrender

The key to having any a success task is a person who does no longer give up. Once you may decide on what you need to do, you have to stick with the selection regardless of what takes vicinity. You ought as a way to perform a little thing and the whole lot feasible to acquire your purpose. Always hold in mind that a success human beings do not cease.

4. Successful People Consider All Their Options

If you want to become a success, you need to recollect all of your options earlier than you make a decision. You must ask what could be useful not handiest to yourself but moreover to the people round you. This manner, you'll short end up at peace collectively along with your selections no matter what the very last results is probably.

5. Independence

Based on my studies, I located that most of the a hit people do not depend upon different humans to make their picks for them. In addition to this, they also do not rely on a person else to take action on their behalf.

6. Confidence

They accept as true with in themselves and stand through their convictions. This dominant trait is what gadgets them apart from some different person inside the international.

7. Successful People Always Have Final Say

They take delivery of pointers but do now not permit exclusive human beings dictate what they want to do.

8. They Live with No Regrets

Living without a regrets is what makes a a success character. No don't forget what errors you've got got made inside the beyond, the first-class way an amazing manner to be successful is to not stay inside the past and actually circulate on. This way, you'll live open to new opportunities and not waste any opportunities that could come your manner.

9. Readiness

Success does not come clean. You want to be prepared to take each possibility that comes your way. You must be prepared to do anything to benefit your desires. Preparedness is the simplest manner a incredible manner to triumph.

10. Never Give Up

Keep on trying till you be successful. The motto for fulfillment. Those who usually win do no longer stop trying till they get results. Also, winners will be predisposed to not take no for a solution. They will do the entirety they likely can to get what they want.

eleven. Take Everything with a Grain of Salt

Successful people do now not allow negativity outline their lives. Of course, you can not please absolutely everyone, but you want to not stay at the negatives. Instead, use these terrible remarks to enhance your self.

12. Do Not Live Your Life Pleasing Others

The 2nd you do that, you could set yourself up for failure and by no means reap something you do.

thirteen. Success Is a Product of Hard Work

One commonplace trait among a hit humans is they paintings difficult. They do not take topics as a right. They typically try to discover ways to decorate themselves. They also are not afraid to test and strive new things. To end up successful, you need to be willing to do the entirety it takes to get what you want. Do not look beforehand to some aspect to reveal up. Make subjects occur.

14. Open-Mindedness

Successful human beings do not restriction themselves to what they assume is proper. They are not afraid to discover one-of-a-kind alternatives and listen to different humans to analyze the manner they're able to resolve issues or make improvements.

15. They aren't Afraid of Change

The most effective element constant on this international is alternate. To succeed, you want to learn how to adapt to trade.

sixteen. Winners Aren't Selfish

The road to achievement is paved with kindness. You becomes a fulfillment in case you recognize a way to percentage what you have with others. You have so that you can impart information as well. Do not hesitate to teach others what you realize. This manner, you will be able to unfold your knowledge and probably make the world a higher area in the long run.

17. They Give Credit Where Credit Is Due

A a hit character is a person who knows the way to complement one of a kind humans for their specific art work.

18. They Bring Out the Best in People

A a fulfillment leader is usually a terrific follower. You need to look at and discover a manner to paintings with a group in case you need to be triumphant.

19. They Are Not Afraid To Make Countless Mistakes

Successful people aren't scared of making errors. They recognize that it's far part of studying and evolving proper into a higher and extra succesful man or woman.

20. Humility

To grow to be successful, you want to famend in that you started out. Do now not permit success visit your head. Always try to assist the human beings who've helped you gain your motive. You might be doubly blessed in case you do that.

Chapter 16: Spartan Style Discipline

Spartans took the whole thing to the intense at the identical time because it got here to electricity of mind and trouble in extremely-present day. They may additionally frequently beat and deliver the children a flogging as a punishment for unsavory behaviors. The youngsters could start their bodily training at age seven after being taken from their dad and mom and located right right into a military program known as the "agoge". This is a real testament to the boy's individualism and to look how properly they're able to feature on their non-public. At the age of twelve they may start to walk barefoot to harden their toes and to workout power of thoughts.

Even although we stay a really outstanding manner of existence from the Spartans, power of mind remains an critical a part of our lives. It takes energy of mind to do your homework, to no longer eat that zero.33 hotdog (or 5th if I am being sincere), and for bodily workout and lots of various topics in existence. So, we may be adjusting the Spartan fashion training of self-control which they did pretty nicely and making it usable in our day and age. I want you to recognize that power of will is the purpose and the paintings that receives performed is a byproduct of that reason. If you take a look at this technique and continuously maintain self-control as your essential aim and the practices you accomplish as facet-accomplishments, you turns into a champion of self and state of affairs, and self-discipline.

Tommy

"Gather up you sorry excuses for Spartan warriors, it's time to expose you into actual warriors." The education instructor stated in an authoritative voice. On todays list we've walking, sword stopping, and spear throwing so get organized.

"Wow." Tommy have become excited and anxious for his education session nowadays. "I without a doubt have professional for my complete existence for this I can't wait!"

Four hours later.

"Tommy we're going to have to paintings for your pace and staying power, you've been closing in every single race." The instructor said in a excessive tone.

"I am doing my fine! I promise I will entice as tons as all of the specific boys… promise." Tommy have become simply beat from his exercise.

"Alright Tommy simply hold on keeping on, unluckily there can be a whipping for you this night for being very last on every race. That must train you to hurry up and to in the long run grow to be a higher warrior."

There changed into a look of fear in Tommy's eyes as he have been crushed in the past, however it became in no way because of his tempo. Alright sir, I might be faster next time we race and I will increase as plenty as be massive and strong similar to my father.

Purpose Filled Life

The purpose of existence is to live a life entire of purpose and to not be frightened of failure. Failure is a steppingstone for your journey and is wanted to get to the vacation spot which you looking for. As prolonged as you live cause driven and keep on following the path (doing subjects that lead you inside the course of your destination in place of away from it) you can be successful.

As an instance, in case your preferred destination is to get into better shape than part of your journey goes to be workout that specialize in cardio. If your quit purpose is better marks in school than a part of your adventure may be analyzing extra and focusing plenty much less on distraction that aren't beneficial.

"Do now not fear failure but instead worry no longer attempting." Roy T. Bennett. Make positive which you understand if you avoid failure and fear failure that your progress may be extensively slowed. The motive of this element is because of the truth in the course of this book you may possibly want to do matters which you haven't accomplished earlier than. Such as spending extra time on effective pursuits and balancing your unproductive pursuits with green ones. If you want to have a few aspect which you do no longer presently have (strength of will) you need to be prepared to do topics that you have not achieved inside the past.

As a Spartan teen locating your purpose wasn't too difficult you were given one possibility which have become becoming a Spartan warrior. This training started once you turned seven years vintage and entered the agoge. In this point in time, you're provided masses of capability functions you would like to fulfill. Say you desired to assist people, you may turn out to be a nurse or a medical doctor or each different career that helps human beings. If you simply loved motors, you may end up an engineer or automobile mechanic or any of the opportunity cute professions. There are such severa possibilities obtainable and I quite recommend searching up a few online exams to discover your motive "Purpose Test or profession quiz" to find out what you're maximum appropriate for. However, in case you already understand what cause you want to meet you'll find out that coming across yourself-disciplined Spartan manner of existence can be lots much much less difficult as might also have your "Why" motive for running in your area.

Tommy

"Alright Tommy all of that schooling has been paying off!" the schooling teacher shouted cheerfully.

"Yeah, I am however feeling like I can run faster however no longer coming in very last place makes me feel higher. Also not being whipped enables me to sleep at night time time.

"Indeed, and if you are feeling like you can run quicker you need to be taking walks as a long way and fast as you can in your off-time. This will assist you to growth your maximum on foot pace and in case you hold at it, you might even emerge as the fastest runner for your age business enterprise!" The training instructor stated in an upbeat manner.

Tommy modified into feeling excited for his future races, "Oh boy! I can't wait to get faster and hold improving!"

Fun Spartan Facts

It changed into a notably not unusual fact that truly one Spartan warrior have become same to at the least numerous other guys from some different country. This surely suggests without a doubt how a protracted way being disciplined can get you.

The Spartans have been excessive about perfectionism. They believed in public shaming as obese citizens had been publicly ridiculed and any babies that have been born deformed could be left to die at Mount Taygetus.

Spartan children may be encouraged to steal as they weren't given a good deal meals or garb and inside the occasion that they had been stuck, they were harshly punished for being caught.

The agoge education machine might teach the thoughts and the frame. Self-situation became the remaining aim of the Spartan schooling system.

Sparta did now not have partitions as they believed that their shields had been their partitions.

They would probable in no manner surrender because it have turn out to be taken into consideration the worst insult to any Spartan man. If a warrior modified into to give up, they might be taken into consideration an outcast through the usage of their society.

If you desired to get a tombstone even as you died, you'll want to each perish in war or in childbirth. Harsh but as an alternative Spartan warriors had been the hardest of the difficult. Absolute monsters even as it came to struggle and power of will.

Spartan infants had been right away bathed in wine after being born. The belief modified into that the weaker infants could probably convulse and die. I needed to wait till nineteen to get dunked in wine due to the fact you understand, criminal consuming age.

Another a part of their unbreakable field have end up that Spartan guys couldn't live with their wives till they had been as a minimum 30 years vintage. These men needed to be inside the training barracks till they have been 30 to be taken into consideration proper Spartan warriors.

30-Day Self-Discipline Plan

This phase of the e-book is meant to reveal words into movement. The exceptional way that permits you to bring together your strength of thoughts is to carry out self-disciplinary moves. The essential idea at the back of this 30-day plan is to lessen the quantity of time you spend on unproductive interests and spend extra time on efficient interests.

You can be required to spend one hour on a inexperienced project or hobby for every one hour you spend on an unproductive interest or undertaking.

Once you achieve the following page and get to writing inside the each day desk, I want you to install writing out your effective and unproductive interests. After that you may be trying to characteristic what number of hours you are spending each day on every this type of interests (written out subsequent to it) and stability your pastimes 1:1 with one hour spent on a efficient hobby for every one you spend on an unproductive interest.

The comments phase is there so that you could make observations approximately how your interests are going preferred. An example remark could be, "Today I spent to hundreds time gaming and not enough time on in reality one in each of my effective pastimes."

You also do now not need to fill in all 5 of the pastimes and when you have greater hobbies to feature than you can write them below the table. Try to attention on the pastimes and obligations which can be taking on the bulk of it gradual because of the reality if you are spending massive quantities of time on the ones unproductive interests, they'll be hurting your self-control ranges.

The extremely good manner to train up your self-control and come to be a real Spartan warrior of field may be to lessen the time you spend on unproductive instant-gratification pursuits and introduce effective hobbies.

As long as you keep on together with your green hobbies it will get much less difficult over the years to live with them and spend greater time on them.

Over the route of the month, you need to be searching out to little by little lessen the time you spend on unproductive obligations and interests and spend that time in a green way. Depending at the extent of strength of mind you need to gather you could both really surrender your unproductive hobbies or hold them carefully. If you are now not capable of control the ones hobbies and time wasters, I suggest sincerely giving them up through the years. If you're able to control the ones hobbies and duties, I recommend sticking to a healthful amount of time spend on them daily.

Productive pursuits / duties

Examples:

• Reading or writing a ebook

• Gardening

• Yoga / stretching

• Weightlifting or aerobic physical sports

• Meditation

• Playing track

• Learning programming

• Artwork

• Sports or karate

• YouTube guides on a way to use Excel

• Fishing

Unproductive and dangerous pursuits / responsibilities

Examples:

•Playing video games

•Watching YouTubers / Twitch streamers playing video video video games

•Smoking / eating

•Pokémon card accumulating (Expensive series conduct)

•Watching any YouTube films that don't convey you closer to your goals

Day One

Chapter 17: Productive Hobbies

Hobby:

1: _____

2: _____

3: _____

4: _____

five: _____

Comments:

Unproductive Hobbies

Hobby:

1: _____

2: _____

3: _____

four: _____

five: _____

Comments:

Day Two

Productive Hobbies

Hobby:

1: _____

2: _____

3: _____

four: _____

five: _____

Comments:

 Unproductive Hobbies

Hobby:

1: _____

2: _____

three: _____

4: _____

five: _____

Comments:

Day Three

Productive Hobbies

Hobby:

1: _____

2: _____

3: _____

4: _____

5: _____

Comments:

 Unproductive Hobbies

Hobby:

1: _____

2: _____

three: _____

4: _____

five: _____

Comments:

Day Four

Productive Hobbies

Hobby:

1: _____

2: _____

three: _____

4: _____

5: _____

Comments:

 Unproductive Hobbies

Hobby:

1: _____

2: _____

3: _____

4: _____

5: _____

Comments:

Day Five

Productive Hobbies

Hobby:

1: _____

2: _____

three: _____

four: _____

5: _____

Comments:

Unproductive Hobbies

Hobby:

1: _____

2: _____

3: _____

four: _____

five: _____

Comments:

Day Six

Productive Hobbies

Hobby:

1: _____

2: _____

3: _____

four: _____

five: _____

Comments:

Unproductive Hobbies

Hobby:

1: _____

2: _____

3: _____

4: _____

5: _____

Comments:

Day Seven

Productive Hobbies

Hobby:

1: _____

2: _____

three: _____

four: _____

5: _____

Comments:

Unproductive Hobbies

Hobby:

1: _____

2: _____

3: _____

4: _____

5: _____

Comments:

Day Eight

Productive Hobbies

Hobby:

1: _____

2: _____

three: _____

4: _____

5: _____

Comments:

Unproductive Hobbies

Hobby:

1: _____

2: _____

3: _____

four: _____

five: _____

Comments:

Day Nine

Productive Hobbies

Hobby:

1: _____

2: _____

three: _____

four: _____

5: _____

Comments:

 Unproductive Hobbies

Hobby:

1: _____

2: _____

three: _____

four: _____

5: _____

Comments:

Day Ten

Productive Hobbies

Hobby:

1: _____

2: _____

3: _____

4: _____

five: _____

Comments:

Unproductive Hobbies

Hobby:

1: _____

2: _____

3: _____

4: _____

five: _____

Comments:

Day Eleven

Productive Hobbies

Hobby:

1: _____

2: _____

three: _____

4: _____

5: _____

Comments:

 Unproductive Hobbies

Hobby:

1: _____

2: _____

three: _____

4: _____

5: _____

Comments:

Day Twelve

Productive Hobbies

Hobby:

1: _____

2: _____

3: _____

4: _____

5: _____

Comments:

Unproductive Hobbies

Hobby:

1: _____

2: _____

three: _____

four: _____

five: _____

Comments:

Day Thirteen

Productive Hobbies

Hobby:

1: _____

2: _____

3: _____

4: _____

five: _____

Comments:

Unproductive Hobbies

Hobby:

1: _____

2: _____

3: _____

4: _____

5: _____

Comments:

Day Fourteen

Productive Hobbies

Hobby:

1: _____

2: _____

3: _____

4: _____

5: _____

Comments:

Chapter 18: Unproductive Hobbies

Hobby:

1: _____

2: _____

three: _____

4: _____

5: _____

Comments:

Day Fifteen

Productive Hobbies

Hobby:

1: _____

2: _____

3: _____

four: _____

five: _____

Comments:

Unproductive Hobbies

Hobby:

1: _____

2: _____

three: _____

4: _____

five: _____

Comments:

Day Sixteen

Productive Hobbies

Hobby:

1: _____

2: _____

three: _____

four: _____

five: _____

Comments:

Unproductive Hobbies

Hobby:

1: _____

2: _____

three: _____

four: _____

five: _____

Comments:

Day Seventeen

Productive Hobbies

Hobby:

1: _____

2: _____

three: _____

four: _____

5: _____

Comments:

 Unproductive Hobbies

Hobby:

1: _____

2: _____

three: _____

four: _____

5: _____

Comments:

Day Eighteen

Productive Hobbies

Hobby:

1: _____

2: _____

3: _____

four: _____

five: _____

Comments:

 Unproductive Hobbies

Hobby:

1: _____

2: _____

three: _____

four: _____

five: _____

Comments:

Day Nineteen

Productive Hobbies

Hobby:

1: _____

2: _____

3: _____

4: _____

five: _____

Comments:

 Unproductive Hobbies

Hobby:

1: _____

2: _____

three: _____

four: _____

5: _____

Comments:

Day Twenty

Productive Hobbies

Hobby:

1: _____

2: _____

3: _____

4: _____

five: _____

Comments:

Unproductive Hobbies

Hobby:

1: _____

2: _____

three: _____

4: _____

five: _____

Comments:

Day Twenty-One

Productive Hobbies

Hobby:

1: _____

2: _____

three: _____

4: _____

five: _____

Comments:

 Unproductive Hobbies

Hobby:

1: _____

2: _____

3: _____

four: _____

5: _____

Comments:

Day Twenty-

Productive Hobbies

Hobby:

1: _____

2: _____

3: _____

four: _____

5: _____

Comments:

Unproductive Hobbies

Hobby:

1: _____

2: _____

3: _____

4: _____

5: _____

Comments:

Day twenty-three

Productive Hobbies

Hobby:

1: _____

2: _____

3: _____

four: _____

5: _____

Comments:

Unproductive Hobbies

Hobby:

1: _____

2: _____

3: _____

four: _____

5: _____

Comments:

Day Twenty-four

Productive Hobbies

Hobby:

1: _____

2: _____

3: _____

four: _____

5: _____

Comments:

Unproductive Hobbies

Hobby:

1: _____

2: _____

3: _____

four: _____

five: _____

Comments:

Day twenty-5

Productive Hobbies

Hobby:

1: _____

2: _____

3: _____

4: _____

5: _____

Comments:

Unproductive Hobbies

Hobby:

1: _____

2: _____

three: _____

4: _____

five: _____

Comments:

Day Twenty-six

Productive Hobbies

Hobby:

1: _____

2: _____

three: _____

4: _____

five: _____

Comments:

 Unproductive Hobbies

Hobby:

1: _____

2: _____

3: _____

four: _____

five: _____

Comments:

Day twenty-seven

Productive Hobbies

Hobby:

1: _____

2: _____

3: _____

four: _____

five: _____

Comments:

 Unproductive Hobbies

Hobby:

1: _____

2: _____

3: _____

4: _____

5: _____

Comments:

Day Twenty-8

Productive Hobbies

Hobby:

1: _____

2: _____

three: _____

4: _____

five: _____

Comments:

 Unproductive Hobbies

Hobby:

1: _____

2: _____

three: _____

4: _____

5: _____

Comments:

Day twenty-9

Productive Hobbies

Hobby:

1: _____

2: _____

three: _____

4: _____

5: _____

Comments:

 Unproductive Hobbies

Hobby:

1: _____

2: _____

3: _____

4: _____

5: _____

Comments:

Day thirty

Productive Hobbies

Hobby:

1: _____

2: _____

3: _____

four: _____

5: _____

Comments:

Unproductive Hobbies

Hobby:

1: _____

2: _____

3: _____

four: _____

five: _____

Comments:

Inspiration

"Hardship often prepares an normal character for an extraordinary future."

-Christopher Markus

"You have strength over your thoughts – not outdoor sports activities. Realize this, and you may find out strength."

-Marcus Aurelius

"Freedom is secured not by way of the use of way of the enjoyable of one's dreams, but with the useful resource of the elimination of choice."

-Epictetus

As we are able to see from those notable fact seeker charges, mastery over self and your very own mind is of excessive importance. Once you have got gotten superb manipulate over your desires and your mind, following your ardour and destiny turns into exponentially less difficult to do.

You'll need a cause to comply at the side of your passions and goals in any other case your fire will probable burn out fast. For instance, in case your important motive is to get into better form, I comprehend that you recognize that it is tough. So, if some thing is hard, we obviously generally tend to keep away from it and do topics that deliver us immediate gratification. Over time exercising will provide us gratification thru seeing our results however, sticking with exercise is the tough component. Ultimately, you'll want a sturdy enough cause "Why" you are following your reason and in this case that "Why" may be, "I want to get into higher form to boom my energy of thoughts, enhance my health, plenty less knee and lower once more ache, and higher sleep." I fairly propose writing all of your reasons, "Why" down and posting it somewhere you may see it everyday like to your bed room or by using the use of your display.

Conquering Cravings

To without a doubt overcome your cravings, you need to cast off what offers you cravings from your location. You will want to practice extreme strength of mind to cope with cravings and understand that with time the cravings will reduce and depart.

Something I pretty suggest in case you beby using way of ordinary cravings is to live busy at a few level in the day. You are 100x a bargain less likely to get robust cravings if you are interested in a hobby which you are into.

If you are surprisingly busy bowling or doing some interest you obtained't need to cope with cravings and thru the surrender of the day you could say, "Wow, that end up smooth!"

 Understand that Spartan warriors found out electricity of thoughts from a totally young age, so they definitely in no way knew some thing else. Learning it in our day and age may be tough however it's also so very worthwhile. Quelling your dreams will increase your power of mind and your freedom (more loose time and also you get to pick out what you do with it.) It definitely is a lovable recognition and harmonious way of living.